TIDES, ELEMENTAL

Helen Taith Curtis began life in Beddington, Surrey, and is now happily settled in Derbyshire, by way of Wales and the Isle of Wight. *Tides, Elemental* is her first collection written over a time of joyous new life and of deep loss; the collection travels these weathers of the heart. She has honours degrees in English (1st class) and German, and it is her love of language and its music that underpins the imagination and emotion of these poems.

ISBN: 978-1-916938-72-4

Cover designed by Aaron Kent

Edited and Typeset by Aaron Kent

Broken Sleep Books Ltd
PO BOX 102
Llandysul
SA44 9BG

CONTENTS

I am certain of nothing but of the holiness of the Heart's affections and of the truth of the imagination.
— Keats

Tides, Elemental

Helen Taith Curtis

Broken Sleep Books

BLITZED
In memory of the oaks, 1987

I woke in chiaroscuro —
cinematic —

a world of tungsten flash,
white arcing.

Outside, the roiling wind rose and boiled,
rumbled late-leaf crowns.

Blind, empty light:
the world sudden, naked —

no canopy,
only a sucking sky

as though these trunks did not bleed,
pale, splintered flesh was not

raw pain, only
my complete negative exposure.

THE NEWS

There is no ordinary moment,
then the news that changes it all.

That's not how it was for me — I said,
not you. I have expected it,

this death. Yet when I got the call,
that now will never be from you,

my reassuring narrative diverged —
we never were two — and here I am,
merely a dreg of you.

FLIGHT, OR AN ABSENCE OF SHADE

Falling asleep into the future, just to find you,
this human cargo hangs in the night.
There are no places to come and see.
I never understood, but here I am.

It was over long ago, but we hung on:
a screen at thirty thousand feet, suspended animation —
I turned atlas pages decades before, in brown relief.
Physical, a distant geography.

I came for you, brother,
the way you brought
yourself home each time,
already ash.

Top of the range, four by four baked earth
flinging dust — a ride to nowhere
but khaki hiding — are guns made from rock?
Redder than I had thought:

ophiolite – nurturing copper, chromites
even where it is brutalised, paraded
against the brilliant sea for a playground,
yachts smacked on cobalt.

The men in the market are an absence of shade,
thobes so finely laundered.
In your pretend suit
you drive us into Jebbel Shams —

words alone are enough, but you are silent.
A football match made of sand
plays out on a far cliff.
I heard you boys shout across the abyss.

On the top, rock is tottery, bare, but the goats are fat.
And a child runs into the road to sell us a carpet —
it is jewelled, it's amber, henna, rust,
and in the market, frankincense

from Boswellia, grown in the Empty Quarter.
I want to inhale your ash.
I think you will be scented,
cinnamon to the tongue's touch.

EVENING, NORFOLK

How many years had we walked here,
by the beck that hems the fen,
the brick mill on the bank stock still,
wherry idling on flat water?

The mill's rusted sails, hang on broad sky
motionless, warblers hushed in the reeds.
Only the silence since your death
lies deeper.

Brother, don't you see my ready canvas,
how I long to sail?
How our images mirror,
limpid on the Bure?

You stared into that water,
transfixed by the illusion
that blinded you
to our reflections;

russet brick, blood-red sail,
we walked beside the beck
where now all
I hear is echo.

A MEMOIR OF THE SEA IN ME

A memoir of the sea in me, a memoir of how
I tried to become the sea, this drought year of all years! A memoir
of how I turned from the tide, and let the land burn me, let the sun
induce hallucination; until I let the unrelenting light speckle me
     like a hen's egg
and I let the fierce gold of fields crackle under my feet
and I let the stink of burning enter my lungs. I let
the river's ochre banks weave their reedy art

in their loopings, their revelations of drowned belfries;
and dared to look at what had been buried
under water. A memoir of knowing thirst and staying
in the light. A memoir of gratitude for breaths
of breeze; of memories of plains of amazement,
and barley flanks of hazy Warwickshire. A memoir
of this year of bodies of sweat melting ripe together;
A memoir of having enough, of slowing
to the pace of creatures of heat.

NOA

A lacuna, a little portal
and the gift arrives.
Shush away interlopers and amaze:
this home of quiet is a holy place.
Here is where the child becomes
in a shrine of her first days.
She arrives a half-born bud
cupped in safe birthing, a trinity
of mother's hush, father-son's primed hands.
They learn of her in wakening eyes
which tell of far-off and will not remember where.
We remove our shoes,
step lightly into her half-awake,
caress her fine-bloom head, speak softly.
We may sit a while,
we may fall in love
with this petal-delicacy, new-blown-in,
then leave this sacred gap in ordinary time
to the blessed parents, while we
tiptoe away, our hands touching.
Or maybe I stay, an interloper, I
am birthing the past in this girl-child,
her eyes still undifferentiated dark, tunnelling her way here.
They watch me weep and wonder why – my hands are sure,
my eyes welcome. In months you will be here,
fully fat and thriving in this love, the thrum of human blood
flowing strong through the trinity of you.

Yet, in the love I feel lies fear for this miniature body sweet and waiting —
fear, for when an arm falters, and her lizard limbs jump into air
or fall, all four, the little beak of mouth shaping itself
to know how a cry of fathomlessness feels —
I wish she would not grow. As though I myself crawl
into the dark cave of her crying mouth
our tiny fingers and thumbs pressed to our face —
still hidden, still safe. Show me, little one,
how you do this – how you thrive – and join the race.
I am like you; I am your wide-awake sense, your brain of images; my
mouth too seeks a shape to cry out darkness:
my eyes are tired of scanning every holy place
to force open other eyes, other hearts.

AMARANTHINE

The year ends   suspended
and I cannot wait the eternity it takes
for one drab leaf   its falling
lounging on its curled back   luxuriating
arms starred out   I am already
gone into the void
a lull   one relentless pause
of the millions suspended in me   or I in them.

So urgent to end before that leaf
touches the wet or desiccates on dry ground   but if I can wait
these turns of absurdity
one leaf's crushing   its face slapped on water
will awake the machine's clatter   the raking of coals
the grinding of colour   lazuli, amaranth.

THE COMFORT OF THORN

The tree is agony, but clings to sky.
Arms reach up, supplicant, and break mid-air.
Now lichen snugs, lime-green.
Grey and dark buds poke — bloodied, thin-spurred.

Fallen branches lie fast to ground
aged by mole-dark fungus clods;
deep cracks, fissures and old splintering —
agony of splitting, the broken writhe of tattered pelt.

But see below: the harbour opens wide as a woman's hips,
where an arm of chalk guides the white ships home
to shelter on a cradling tide —
or line up, drawn on a child's page too high.

Pinks, blues, sandy-ochres; greys
and bright fern-green floodwaters
lie on farmland up the Yar
their marshes, mirrors for sky.

Here, on hawthorn's aged limbs,
we fastened your bright flowers, my boy,
as gulls hung crosses on sapphire blue,
we headed back, bent to wind.

By thorn-brakes we slowly descended,
two gulls, slow flapping,
wrapped a comfort
and carried us down.

ANGLING

So you fish
enchantment
into the tungsten stream

and pierce our viscous skin
with hook and
enticement

now a crowd
of writhing muscle
a bundle of slung darkness

black tunnels against the sundance stream
we open wide for you

and are taken in

yet in a flash
scales fall into sunlight —
it's you that's hooked

                    iridescent
                    amethyst, emerald
                    our flesh, rose-blush

a trick of course

we bite on every shining, stinking thing
you dangle before our flat fish-eyes.

THE TUNNELLED HEART

There has been a tide that would not turn,
but battered at the hatches
of my selves before they blew.
And I shored up and stayed shored up.
Such destruction is incompatible with flow.

Only, I have heard its echoes once again
but deeper underground,
like those old London rivers
whose names reverberate from culverts:
Wandle, Tyburn, Fleet.

The race slowed, enough
to roll us in with the formless things,
enough to fashion rudimentary hands
to mould a leech, a leaping in the gut,
then a shoal. Nameless imagos

puddled here, turned over,
thrown back, or warmed.
Because this time, I was not alone,
but accompanied in the tunnelled heart,
where the tide flows both ways.

TULIP

You seemed to be born blind.
At first in a chipped pot, in frosted compost,
your leaves pined — jaded limp swords.
Fingering in, I could find no core,
nothing that might bloom.

So we passed the days.
You grew lankier with the light.
But still, unpromising.
Until I thought a slit of pink discernible,
where your heart might be.

I allowed no hope, only acceptance
that you were to be nothing at all.
But, through those barren days, you persisted.
Threw up, one morning, a wavering stem,
balancing on the head. A bud.

The cold returned. The spring was false
dawn to newly-returned swallows.
Early celandines hid their premature suns.
But your stems, veering like snakes uncoiling
half-blind, sought the light, insistent.

Last Wednesday, it was. I stepped outside to find
a pair of fires, two fires or stars of fire — you flamed
sudden and shockingly scarlet — waxed petals flung wide
open — and your heart nothing timid, but bristling black
round the tiniest triune sun.

BECOMING SNOW

What bliss this is! Before, the sky froze open,
every last bit of matter visible, all its edges
and people and me, and no softening of a blemish;
and everything you say would be so loud, but now!
Look at this eiderdown; the snow gathers in feathers
to fluff the mucky, hard-edged world.
I have no fear. I talk to the neighbour, knowing my words
muffle in the whiteness, knowing she cannot see
beyond the crystal coat I'm gathering on me; knowing
she is becoming no more than a snow-person,
the same as every other stumpy, slowed down
and altogether beautiful snow person.
Noise no longer clatters off walls and windows; this buffer
of snow is for wrapping bodies and spirits,
for disappearing and appearing, for leaving
only footprints that soon fill to vanishing, leaving
only petals of mock orange, camellia, gardenia.

AFTER EPIPHANY

How to make it through this narrow place,
to a slice of barely-there light
and a year's harvesting. All that has bloomed
in us: gaudy wrappings, thick and sickening layers,

now shrinks through the gap: a slot,
a letterbox compressed into the dark
glut of crimson stuff, stifling —
resisting the thin promise, or stripped to fit.

But, the light of January is a pleasant thing.
Peridot, no scarlet merriment.
The warm-blood mare still crops the field,
pearl skies spread high and wide, unwritten.

BULB

Unpromising pyramid, plastic green
breaks your skin, and
from your tight jaw, a lick
of sickly pink.

This, from parchment flake
a dry, weightless husk
buried in the misery
of winter soil — and yet —

your strength. No need
to be seen or heard in the dark,
though you might desiccate in grief —
you're quiet about it.

And here you are, even now,
when the world spawns plague —
you burst from dirt,
scent the air to pull in bees,

you know the life you bear —
its energy, its air,
and we pale for the want of it.

AND UNDER MY FEET

On the road, khaki-drab
hover of golden apples,
late lights in the yew.

Oak clings on, copper
country dancers, late to leave,
still full of frills.

Silver birch coin clinks.
There's a stink everywhere, lying
water or something dead.

Hawthorn leaves, papery.
A rivulet creeps, snail-like.
Everything drips.

In the yard, a tap
bandaged with an oily rag,
is alight with silvers.

Horses steam in a field
that will never make hay again;
old man's eye of moon seeps, rheumily.

Muck boots clog,
a tractor stands askew in the ruts,
slop-swilling its wheels.

Gulls blown in from the coast,
grubby in the mud with crows,
find fieldfare to snaffle, red spindles.

Ashes are bone now
and on the verge,
asteroid thistles: blue-green.

And under my feet lies ragwort,
in little muddied suns
that refuse to go out.

CALF SONG
to Ninsum

Dam-kin enclosed in this high field
in peace, you are stone stillness
milk-white, flint-hipped and humped —
in peace, sound low our secret speech.

In love, bend your wave-lined neck to me
patient tongue lap my curled poll;
in love, bathe me with deep-lashed eye —
flood-waved, my spirits rise.

In courage, I suckle from pillowed bosom
ever-fed from source;
in courage I lean under your swayed heft —
field walls fall at my hands.

In mourning, I take the mountain path
our grieving, one night of howl;
I hold in my heart your warm stone side
your tender eye,
patient tongue, full breast —
your sweet liquors of Paradise.

Ninsum – Lady Wildcow, mother of Gilgamesh

OWEN

This baby in my arms
is becoming as we watch;
a damp-wing fledgling.
His eyes, peaty pools
floating;
just once resting on my face,
newly shucked from his soft shell,
raw in the blue light.

He breathes quickly,
his bird-bone ribs pulsing hard
as though he must keep the rhythm going,
not knowing
nature does that for him
in some miraculous bellows instinct
that will last a lifetime.

His skin, the silken lining of a chestnut husk,
puckers in tiny furrows of effort;
already thinking his own thoughts,
expressed in an interior look
and a sound,
like the tiniest command.
Testing, testing.

CRUCIBLE

Framed in oak the bark to bear you
boards cut where the green-crowned king
bowed low; offered himself
a vaulted ark, big-hearted.

Within,
limbs of willow cradle raked bones
sister fingers braid a creche for you;
with memory of water, peel and shed
the unsuitable suit;
lie my dear in lattice-weave
rocking, lapping, weeping.

Extinguished
as your glorious hour receded,
burn again in frankincense
harvested from your red-bone desert
Boswellia, Sallalah
the tree's dripped tears
coil smoke around you, tendrils
soothe, soothe – balm for your flayed skin

almond flowers for your lips
blue hibiscus for your eyes
so your children will know you.

Your essence rises, rich and fragrant;
oud of agarwood – born of corruption
Aquillaria
precious resin from black infection
in the heart-wood
now transmuted.
Breathe now, dear brother
the air in here is sweet.

Rest now, oak bears all
blood, bone, breath and grace.

EARTHED

Nothing is still   a hanging gull
snipes on rock   its feathers blading in the breeze

skeleton fireweed spirals white   dark fists of flutter
are rooks or leaves   late this autumn.

one young herring gull   bark-speckled   crucifix wings
out-spans its holy parent
until a gust collapses his greedy geometry

one last violet in the chine   one last melting of wings
dog-days detritus of many lives   most unlived
spin litter

emptying trill   emptying stink
of tainted brook trickling in the cliff
on its knees to the sea   where it is whipped renewed moon-whisked
to white peak cleaning

rocks are slimed   barnacled   seething
and we – we are planted, forked, upright for a reason.

EXPOSURE

Only fixed light kills,
subject to interrogation.
Burns you naked in its forensic gaze.

Lands are baked to red-bone rock,
ossified by the burning eye.
All forms drained of suppleness

as day-sun coruscates and pavements
hit out. I take a mallet to its baked glaze:
the smack of annunciation.

White blaze blinds by revelation.
A freeze-frame seer imprisons
hollowed-out souls in striplight.

Lingering in this solar glare:
stasis examines you to death.

FALSE MOON

Luna
light in moth's wing
the lumen and the snuff
wing paper to powder
desiccate   a stain on fingertip.

Phototaxis lure to detour
veer from moon by false light
moth's geometric genius fails
spirals inward tantalised

gazes at fake moons
forgets to eat
dies in dazzle.

Moth wing peel
from weight of body
brief the life, the pouf

is all you were body just meat.

THE WATER ITSELF

I

Our words, tossed lightly on this counterpane sea,
are coined for you from silted eyes.

Meshed with blindness, peeled
from wiry nerves, cast

as clink to rivers, that flicker
and dull, rippled to weather.

We are none of this, only
water, the body of water.

II

And all the way home, I heard the voices —
the tinkling of buoys far out at sea —

or memory, whose fearsome
coast is not the craggy shore,

but an echoed
retort of featureless grey.

But we are far out at sea, have wound
each other in weeds of words

softly, like webs, then thicker, thicker:
the inevitable tidal drawl.

III

First, crack the fatted coat to emerge,
a pressed, encasing flesh

lobbed on rock and then released.
A burgeoning muscle

speechless in the swell and lull,
yet do not stay –

with sea-wounded feet limp out
with me, ignited and alive.

GORSE

Flung from Jupiter's finger, arrow points,
little suns, flicked stars speckling the heath
onn onn onn
over Breton shores we flash chrome yellow
blaze of furze, beacon-bright for sailors
wreck-threatened in sea-fret.

Our leaves,
crackled baskets of spine-weave
make a cradle for beetle, adder, slow-worm, toad,
for shivering spiders strung out on a line.

Husky, drab, our star-thorn nests light at a spark
cut and scrub and punk for fire-starters
we burn brightest at Beltane!
in cadmium flare of aromatic oils —

or race our flames across the heath,
faster than the witches' hares can run.
Our pods burst black, crack the sky open — scatter-gun
seed spreads new constellations.

Conflagration is short-lived,
for here, tender green,
we uncoil gentle as any fern —
and lambs come with their flinty mouths,
chaw-chaw on intimate shoots.

And softly now, we can be your rest;
end of day, weary, under pillows of mist
we pattern down, cloak Welsh hills — patchwork
yellow-painted gorse, purple heath, ling
a counterpane.

GROWING ROOM

As though emaciation
is only on the outside   as though words
                                    can tell it all — or, at all

for a child made of language
each shade, inflection, tone, noted
terminology, insinuation   parroted.

                                    The only language not known
                                    was her own, her books in the
                                    mouths of others.

Though dry, yet air is left   still
unformed, unbreathed

                                    a little space
                                    but there's time.

When all the tongues spoke
worlds were created   not the hop hop from sound to
                                    sound like hussocks on the
                                    runneled moor, but interlace
                                    of roots, a weave

gathered round more friendly
self to self   so the starved centre could
                                    exhale, inhale, fattening with
                                    kindness of closeness.

HIS SHAPELY HEAD

white sky, white

tide sucks in slurps pukes out a carcass   wave on wave on wave
stranded, wave-taken / sea-swallowed / rumbled
caught in tangled lines - your red lines dear.
White east light.
How did the great meat of you fly away so lightly?
Smashed bird
your gannet guts
strings of wrack red black

       andthegreatwingsthecrashedslam

wings
     all   angles   of   mechanical
                    failure inarticulate
the bent   slammed foils
           the broken   unspoken

And, oh! The shapely head.

On chalk white boulders

white rock   white rock   white rock   ranks of
black fly   skull seamed   ruby veined spread   beach fleas
eye socket   wobbly zig zag   of neurons, corraline   write the rock
      of a shaky god   unintelligible

HOOKED

Smack of splash,
scaly back,
rake of bones,
a trick, a hook,
a rack, slack,
prick —
a fish.

I CRY THE TIN OF YOUR SCALES

As though a minnow
in river's ravelling — leeched white feet,
dead-man's toes, in water-glass, tender
as the salmon's underbelly

plumbs weedy wraps, mud-lurk depths,
downspirals in concentric rings
where light liquifies, mauve, bronze,
and a cushioning quiet rocks —

at the tipping point, you flip —
slip the water's edge, silt-slimed:
spectrum-reflected in a breeze-whipped stream
coin-clink ellipses break the skin.

Dare-darting little fish — keep moving
your metal scales cut by skimmed stones.
Flighty river thing, zig-zagging on scrim,
tipping on the water's edge,

I cry the tin of your scales.
In the torrent-roar of culvert tunnel,
concrete-carcassed and insignificant —
minnow, you roll, untethered, guttered,

til undaunted, you emerge —
spat out platinum — a plucky fish.

IMAGE

I paint a house
destroyed, but the frame
remains around
a green and gold Arcadia
I paint within.

And the gape is the bone
of my face ablaze
and the land beyond
a song
I have yet to sing.

IN-CARCERATION

Transposed   I learn again to smoke.
The only way to breathe there   was to blow
hoops of me to peer through to burn away
the greasy taste of fear   observe
little stacks of ash in place of gaze
take off dove grey   in circled exhalation.

I breathe myself absent   in this strange place
spiral away from this oval table   and rise above
these strangers who I seem to know shush out molecules of me
grey white   ghost white   into air to not be here.

Wreaths to ride in I made us woven in atmosphere
purified in burning   I learned it young
to be subsumed in cool blue shroud
scented white flake of my burning mouth eyes
little tipped piles of hate

and my self   evaporated over and over in spiral writing
as though these trails of scribbled air
wove a carpet to ride away   barely there
(and you refused
and the last halting breath you never took
but stopped dead one night far from home   and alone
and I here, waiting).

I incinerate myself white ash they left me
tiny tipping stacks of cinder   each time
the fire due to ignite   snuffed
at the oval table and your face and my
escape in shame and dismay of smoke.

IN SOLUTION

The fields flare sulphur and the sky —
horizon is no more and the sun does not blind or brighten
the vetch or the chamomile
but runs in rivers over the land.
Materiality of creature, leaf
dissolve to soul and all is gold of eternity.

MORUS BASSANUS: SHADOW ON THE SEA

straight through the heart of me again and again and again
— Morus Bassanus, Northern Gannet

I shape-shift
          only for her
my white sail, wave-wandering lady
her no-fuss, no-time flight
how she stills the air, sea stalker.

It's the murder of me, but I never lose sight
of her high cross, diamond-cut in sky,
and wild work keeping her pattern
on this restless clinker-scrim.

She needs me.
Me, her mark, her muddy footprint.

Calm days, I take it easy, a little drift, flip-
flop on my back watching her soft breast above;
or, when sea murmurs and breezes ribbon the water,
I dance my ballerina arms outstretched
embrace of her lovely white sway.

Cross-currents
          wind against tide
I'm in pieces.   Ripped
triangles of my substance
slap on sides and peaks of waves.
I stumble over edged ellipse,
peel off
I'm shattered.

still I watch I watch my darling's
laser-eyes stall — a fraction
silver victim shoals her thrill

I do my best to gather myself, assimilate
my shape, darken, sharpen
        X marks my spot;

powering down, she comes
with great crewel beak
now my rush to keep up
parallelogram, rhombus, fold, fold
pantograph-mechanical
she angles down   and
arrow-plunge

NEGLIGEE

I speak through thin lips —
my words, ashy foils
blowing in bitter air.

Hard teeth fend the flow,
brittle guards of the gateway,
tongue shoved back in throat.

> *Was I, too, nothing but death?*
> *shadow-danced, unaudienced*
> *secret ballerina*
>
> *of day's pink interplay —*
> *shapes and shades of dancing feet,*
> *gauzy on a gunmetal sky,*
>
> *pirouetting blind,*
> *suckered into the dead-end maze*
> *of your unseeing eye?*

I traipse attics, step
in dust-warm vaults, grey breathing
rummage furred loft,

unwrap cobwebs,
lift off thin copies of skin,
fling flimsy selves on boards —

worn duds, negligee;
ballerina's cooped-up years
diamonds blade the sight

eyes weep copper salts,
arabesque to a blown-glass moon
my molecules of light.

NO SWEET FAREWELL OF SEA-GLASS

I will walk into the sea
with no drama;
whale grey wave-humps
and no sweet farewell of sea-glass.

Few shall see me
shingle-slip.

The sun is all glare — a haze of the sea,
and it nauseates;
mutterings, like incessant fleas
infesting.

I will be rolled
like stones in a drum
muffled, as the dead-eyed cold
stuffs ears, nose, mouth.

I only wait for the binding weed
to loosen, slacken off —
so that I can tie up the ends
around my loved ones in rough bows;

then, with the out-breath of the tide
the deep sea's last gasp
I will rise and howl against the drag,
'no sweet farewell for broken sea-glass.'

AFTER PIECES / I WOULD BURY YOU IN AIR

Kindness of trees, bear the bloat of him
drowned in his own salt tears.
Lift him in blessing, no rot, no seep
only tender, dust-blown wind.

Serpent of ivy, grasp on trunk, hold him secure
grip to ground   *snake-skin a suit to shed, ever new*

Morning web spider, string the gorse
quilt threads, a cradle   *spin, fly; cocoon on a line*

Weaver bird, gift your nest, embroidered cup
to collect quenching dew   *your sea-thirst is boundless*

Heartwood, split for the freedom he needed wheels
for fate's turning, for returning   *splayed, nailed, the eternal round*

Magpie, drop by the bright key
to spring many doors, and close them   *under-dungeon, key thrown*

Sleek scull of skins, row the night lake stern-lit
with beetle's glow   *your skull, thin-skinned, bone-breached scuttled*

Now air plays music on sinew, chord
kind wind rattles finger-bones, a prayer   *a pardon*

OBSERVING STAR-MOSS IN MILLDALE

See how a universe of stars implodes in green
and what scattered galaxies converged
to pimple these stone walls with beaded moss
like the sharpest stars in an earthbound night.

OPUS

This is purgation of life
strip-light slow motion, my head
a monotone of bloodless space   open plan   partition
manufacture of human —
white shirt   whiteboard   white light
white out.

So, below, my love in my hand
and tunnelling and tunnelling
leading on to way after way —
we go fearlessly in dread — and at the end
the monotonous drab *does* clatter on us
as pyrites metallic grey and fake.

There is nothing down here, nothing down here.
Where are the colours, the fabulous fermentations, if not here?
Un-fluorescent
a gannet that will not fly again, blue-white body of a poisoned
dab, green shed shells of crab, a clinging on of tentacled things for
fear of drifting.
Swans glide on water barely a ripple and not a smut, not a blot —
nothing touches them in their mirror-swim — not a jot of debris
or mucky scrim. Stand away — distance blends all life to grey —
grey rock, grey sea, grey islands.

Along the brimstone shore, birch drips sulphur on granite faces
– the scars, quarried contributions, opportunities for heather,
lichen, a sundew on an angle of ledge, moss in stars; where men

hacked, iron rails track and strut to the sea and godwits, snipe
stalk shallows there or a yellow throated shag hangs out his fustian
to dry.
The restless sea! Its mercury riddling itself in the body of the bay
— and sandpipers switch foam— white knife-black as they blade
in spray. And on the ruby shore, washed-up kelp ropes quiver
burgundy with tumbled crabs and the mass churns in fleas and
shrimps and mites. The turgid grey that lulled curlews quiet is
cracked by bright wind that spatters lace on laundered sand and
clams open in panic. Sanderlings agitate and hooded crows gather
on churning banks with their sulphur stink. Northern divers
stretch their necks and plunge again.
Light and cloud run around in games where stillness is death.
There is no direction.

Our feet in this teeming stain ochre; the repeat in leaf, in feather,
in scaly claw; in crystal, shell and weedy cell; crab loosens its
carapace and cinnabar seeps in our white bodies and blood
thrums — nowhere to go and nothing to know.
So slowly the tentacled ribs uncoil — release
beads of quicksilver in full moment of quiver
right here in this morass, in this crustacean haven, inside this
body of salts. Evening quiets and the tide is coming in over the
hills with the swimming birds.

PYRE

When rage is undertow,
slack, slag-black and drag of shingle — ignite
the spoil-heap — conjure
flame
to leap, a living sea,
its roiling peaks whipped high.

Cast your curses to dance in tongues
violet, gold
not agape like clotted fish.

As brilliant pyres flung heroines
to bespatter night sky,
make fire, transmute bleak death,
make flame.

SAP

It's when you speak
to the bark and not the tree
we weep in our pulpy core

our freshening green
curls in bilious bud
or drops, unknown.

SEA-DAM

Sea — slate-grey, weary, fake-waved to hurl in hope,
you deceived us. You tempted us
and our mother fell for it.

Cold, iron-clad, eternal bloody vastness,
you call, your sirens and selkies
you called from wrinkled skin — a lead-lined fate

and men go down in ships and the women wail
and wait for maroons thudding
regurgitate consecrate

                        lost souls   to your
                                   empty embrace.

Fooled in our mother's womb, we heard the tide's pulse you and I —
as though there was life in the hump and heave, as though
the husssh was a soothe
and not just a shadow gone to nothing
as the shifting sea shadows only itself.

No vessel ever held you, greening or rusting
in your gun-metal suit —
white flakes were all of you we threw to the tide.

SEEDS OF SILENCE

Wizened seed of Ammi,
tiny tomb, stone-bound pip,
you lost your wings,

yet on striated shell remains
a moment of flight, etched
memory of parachute.

Scratchy little pyramid —
snapped off and sealed —
what ancient secrets do you hold?

When the time is right,
you will loose your parachute strings
and out-blossom your white silks,
blooms for bees,

lacy garments for your Queen.

SHOALS FOR A REQUIEM

In through walls of sand elaborations, elevations, spires, gargoyled
and curlicued, terracotta scribbled on blue — it was a saint from
the north brought the seas and transformation; red mid-land mud
bloomed miracles.

Shoals swim in a glass kaleidoscope where the west doors fling
open a cobalt-gold flood like a romantic war, and we, the faithful,
bow in our heroic hospitality to it all. A thousand swarm in
the sea of faith that crumbles and rebuilds by tides: Eastertide,
Passiontide, and the relief of not smiling.

Uncapped heads bob in the flotsam with slivered fish of turquoise,
yellow, rose; paisley of grey and pastel of saints that drip on
praying heads, coughing heads, high-voiced choirboy heads. I am
every note of the choir as without the rest there is misattunement.

Nobody cries and nobody joins the line snaking round pews,
through apses, synapses, past the empty chancel, avoiding the
high altar as it's only a death not the resurrection.

Nothing here matters because, at a chasm, the organ blasts,
rattling the bones and brains of the quick and the dead. Stained
glass saints vibrate. Shocked virgins vibrate. Marble flags and
tombs of dead bishops vibrate and a thousand damp-eyed
peace-makers sniffle and cough and fumble for change for paltry
offerings and flap their mouths and approximate the hymn.

Under the mud floor you hear the murmur of rippling water echoing, familiarly, in a landscape of flooded valleys and sudden rock walls.

All of us not touching on the same sea-bed; flickering fish shoal in the high windows - so our song is drained and air and wet skin stained and this, now, makes the difference as we turn one at a time and en masse to meet in deep condolence and the smiling brings tears that shimmer with a bright grief like the end of time eyes of fish just before the hook bites.

And in the end, you do drink from the chalice; you, parched, take the sacred vessel as the stone- dead priest sees into your ridiculous game. Only, when your lips touch its pilgrim rim, and you tip towards essence, the nectar has vanished, and there is only dry wine to roll around your useless tongue.

THE LAST WORD

Slow beep heart trace and the ward grey-dimming at night — you,
a husk, hanging on to the fury that keeps you breathing

I'm the only one here though,
the men couldn't stay.
I'm here – and still
                    you breathe and any moment you will say — what has
been on your lips
five decades.

                    I cannot touch your sallow skin the shame I have
                    let you become this chicken bone, wingless,
                    lame dead thing.

Your lips in unreadable O, more ineffectual blankets — where is
your hot blood? Your bright sharp-beak brain?
I fear to touch you still, clawed hand —

                    but Oh God I love you, mother
                    Oh God, what is this death?

I meant to sing your spirit home
hand you over to Jesus myself
when the time came.

Green-sag curtain and your breathing
                    is suffering, the nurse said just so I know everyone
can hear.
So why force drips into rejecting veins?

I said this all along. No, I tried —
and every cry was in private.

Shadows slide from under the bed
ghostlight gleams out your umbrage

        I'm watching your desiccation.
                Body fluids seep in bright yellow bags.
        This thirst curses me.

I can give you no cup, no sponge of bitter water, only call the too-
late, word-wasting priest.

The last rites can't redeem
this wordless reckoning.
I look on, that's all,
sipping my tea.

THE WARMTH OF YOU

No one is here
but the heat of you

the meat of you —

and I wouldn't mind the cleaver
knife and blood

or the sluicing of fluids
and the deluge, the wading
up to our eyes in saline.

Only no one is here
but the warmth of you
your hand laid on mine, custodial.

Your skin, circulation throbbing
rosy, and the hairs on your wrist
still dark —

only your silence is ice
and I boil inside
like a fat stew of all
the odds and ends hacked off —

until you try to put the lid on
and the salt, the blood
scald as I empty and empty.

THROUGH THE WOODS

Blood in January, the hunter vanished
spoor dropped here, and here, in bare white wood

and hemming the edges of city spoil
sweet, dark wine for women of the road

restless light teases the keeper of the keys
rusting bunches hang, heavy on winter bough

thicket dark and deep, bow-bending
conceals and guards the secret cleft

spindle, elder, ash and yew.

yellow-gold of Celtic coast
gutters and sparks a crackling blaze, flame of furze

railways embroidered purple-stitching
never say die – never say die – never say die

Strong arms raise up his broad, green crown
all hail staunch king, big-bellied host

on little floats and barks of silver grey
usher the weepers – sweep them downriver

gorse, buddleia oak and willow

Lemon lambs' tails, bright on blue
wand-waving, dip divine for water

from the mountain, mantle of berry
feast for hungry flocks, journeying

virgin promise, demurely petalled
blushes moist and pink in modest leaf

ladies grey in full-frilled skirt
rustle their young uphill in husky shade

hazel, rowan, apple and beech

Too-sweetness of brief life, a swoon
flute of Pan, brown-sickening

gossip with the water, little games
of cones and twigs-in-ripple

thicket of thorn, catch the felon
keep him there, make him swear

night-shining, gateway to winter
white bark peels, shivers, platinum

lilac, alder, prickle-eye bush, silver birch

TIDES, ELEMENTAL

On the lintel-edge of action
Static, you are as a mariner
stranded on languishing ship
where tides have ceased
and waters slacken, brackish —
you thirst.

you have seen by sun's sudden eye, too late
the tomb, the trap, the noonday glare
that seals the sight.

Then weep for the sweet decrepitude of home.

Though offered a place to stay —
you were warned
that nectar would thicken with flies
and oceans' silver shiverings, lilac-gilled
would fester and spoil —
you thought it courage to linger in the sun
your many men fattening under your command —
you forgot to seek out the night
to turn your ship to the tide!

The gods know unless the waters gaze at sister moon
there is no motion.

Seas stand, an oily stink
a ship adrift and every man, woman, child
falling silent in tongue and wit

as salt drinks them dry —

I can tell you, unless you turn
from greedy glare to moon's renewal
stasis
will droop your sails, see your crew
become spirit before your sight.

***

Step from that place, yes
furies will do their worst — still there's no avoiding
devouring Scylla whose greed
makes carnage of all affections
or the swirling abandon of Charybdis —
who leaves you alone at last —

Your body will flail and pray agaun under the empty,
blameless sky,
but unseen, gods speed you on, over the wine-dark sea
to your grown child, your patient home.

Hear me! Do not take your eyes from moon!
Weep and flow with Selene's tides —

I can tell you, you will be guided
and tempest is elemental.

TO SALVAGE THE HEART

Depth-charge the years, swim
as a mermaid, slip-reeling streams —
you know these oceans,
their cold, clandestine threats.

Daylight dies, a dream
of fields and flowers;
your scaly tail flails
you acquiesce, obedient to undertow.

Here on edge of legend, sunk
in a sea king's cave unfathomable
lies your buried heart — so tender for lack of tending —
the dive has been so long, so hard.

The water's limit sparks crystalline
drapes you in mariner lace: woman, emerge,
in star-sharp refusal to abide, bloodless in tide.
Your marrow runs warm in the sun —

mortality brightens skin, eyes;
water becomes a memory of flood,
and if the tide does stop turning —
eternal is just a word from the hymnal.

WHITE BIRD FLOWN

Of course, I reach
for my white bird, flown.
For I only ever saw him
a sky-sketched outline   in blue
to slip into.

YOU WERE ALREADY DEAD!

You think annihilation is new?

You will either be obliterated, or you won't.

Close your eyes.

How often have you smacked, jagged, into that star, struck through the glass with a fist? And the sharp dark beyond?

But then again, you may choose to sidestep – behind the maroon curtain to watch the sea of lilac, sulphur floodlight bobbing with the bodies of the others – and, I know, they may do unspeakable things, but you are only an actor; you will feel nothing.

Don't you know yet – you chose a walk-on part in all of this? Understudy, many roles you have been cast. And what do you think the changing light is? And the faces you half know, who are not as they were – because the play is underway! And you have not moved from your place in the wings, while watching them morph – magenta, lime, in the floodlights, dancing.

And, don't you remember the high-arched organ loft, its scent of must? The music that flowed from the stained beauty of his hands, his swaying head so delicate, like a bud? You were already dead then! The women put a robe on you, much too large.

The last time you extinguished, you were happy. She came for you in the blue, remember? They all came to see you off, see you rise up, illuminated, dissipating like snuffed sparkle. Do you remember? You waved.

Just sleep. Sleep if you can.

HIBERNATION SONG

It's late afternoon and early sloe froths,
unknowing that the world has emptied.

A lapwing flashes an emerald nape —
as if unnoticed, while

thready trees stitch rust-rising acres
and the gate, red tractors fade, outdated.

Ploughed fields bump up dream-shadows,
ruck up naked, waiting, for the yellow rape.

The hedgerow's brutalised by mechanised blades,
ramparts of thorn-arms buckle, break,

crack – and expose
white, obscene pulp.

Furred bees stir
while we hibernate

in sterile space
as though we could be separate.

FLIGHT, OR AN ABSENCE OF SHADE
Reprise

And somehow the khaki road
led us here – rose desert, sharp sky.

Night and sand become villages of wool,
woven shawls, canopies.

And still I have seen no green —
only ochre, terracotta I've soaked in.

The sun burns cracks where warm
blood spreads in seams.

I know why you never left:
what looks barren, offers up home.

ACKNOWLEDGEMENTS

My thanks go to the editors of the following journals, who have published poems included in this collection: *ArtemisPoetry, Dreich, Ink, Sweat and Tears, The Poetry School* (blog) and *Oxford School of Poetry Reviews*.

Thanks to Dr Kirsten Norrie of The Oxford School of Poetry, for her inspiration, guidance and invaluable support in the creation of *Tides, Elemental*.

Thanks to Aaron Kent and *Broken Sleep Books* for having faith in this book and putting it out into the world.

And love and gratitude to my husband and life-partner, Richard for his cheerful help with all of it; and to our children and their children, lights of our lives.

LAY OUT YOUR UNREST

www.ingramcontent.com/pod-product-compliance
Lightning Source LLC
Chambersburg PA
CBHW030855090426
42737CB00009B/1243